My HEART SPEAKS

Phillis Birmingham

ISBN 979-8-89043-464-7 (paperback)
ISBN 979-8-89043-465-4 (digital)

Christian Faith Publishing
832 Park Avenue
Meadville, PA 16335
www.christianfaithpublishing.com

Printed in the United States of America

DEDICATION

I dedicate this book of poems to my God, my Savior and Lord. You spoke, in such a gentle voice, the poems and the sayings to me; and I pray that within this book others will hear Your voice speaking to their heart. I want to dedicate this book to the most wonderful gifts that God has blessed me with—my two daughters, who, in many ways, have been the inspiration for me to write this book and show them that no matter what, it's never too late to follow your dreams. To my grandkids, I love you so much. You are grand for a reason. Thank you for your unconditional love and being the voice of care when I wasn't feeling too good mentally. And most of all, my great granddaughter—you are so precious to your GiGi. Always remember you have always made my heart smile. God knew you would be my sunshine always. I love you with all my being. To God be the glory for all my blessings.

WHERE DO I GO FROM HERE

Where do I go from here? Through the pain and the heartache and all my fears, where do I go from here? My past seems to be a constant reminder of my future, and when my footsteps are unsure about the path I need to take, where do I go from here? My joy has become a river of sadness that drowns my emotions and consumes my thoughts day after day. Where do I go from here? **LORD, I HEAR YOUR VOICE** telling me that in Your arms is where I need to be. For in Your arms is where all my pain and heartaches diminish, and all my fears and doubts are put at ease. In Your arms, my past becomes a flickering light that disappears as my future shines as bright as the sun. In Your arms, You direct my path. I no longer lean on my own, for You make my footsteps sure. In Your arms, I have joy unspeakable; and I'm surrounded by a sea of love that lifts me up and renews my mind. Where do I go from here? **IN MY FATHER'S ARMS.**

I'M HERE

If you need a pair of ears to listen, **I'M HERE.**

If you need shoulders to help you bear your pain, **I'M HERE.**

If you need arms to hold and comfort you, **I'M HERE.**

If you need a gentle kiss to wipe away your tears, **I'M HERE.**

If you need a heart to understand and care, **I'M HERE.**

I'm here whenever you need me, my dear friend, **I'M HERE.**

HAPPY FATHER'S DAY

You were the one who taught me all about life. When life's ways knocked me down, Your strong hands picked me up and helped me stand on my feet. When I needed comfort, Your tender touch comforted me; and You gave your all so I would lack nothing. You loved me unconditionally when I went the wayward way. Yes, You are the best dad a child could be blessed with.

HAPPY FATHER'S DAY,
LORD

TAKE ME UP TO HEAVEN

This letter was written back in 2012 by my granddaughter, who is now eighteen. She was eight years old when she wrote this poem. I knew God was speaking to her heart at the time, and so I am going to share with you her poem.

> God take me up to heaven I want to see your white robe. Your angels or full of peace and peace is full of love and love is full of God. And God is in our hearts, and he protects us from the dangerous things in our head and body. Our body is full of peace, and our feet is full of action, and God has the strength to fight the dangerous things.

GOOD-BYE, HELLO

Good-bye to loneliness,
Hello to never being alone.
Good-bye to sadness,
Hello to joy unspeakable.
Good-bye to sickness,
Hello to divine health.
Good-bye to confusion,
Hello to a sound mind.
Good-bye to fear,
Hello to boldness.
Good-bye to lack,
Hello to provision and abundance.
GOOD-BYE,
Self
World
Devil
HELLO,
Father
Son
Holy Spirit

IS IT TOO LATE

Is it too late for my dreams to become reality? Is the person **I AM** all I'm going to be? Are the whys in my life never to be answered? Will I ever truly be free? I want to know. I really need to know—is it too late for me? Deep in my heart lies the answer: no. For You, Lord, hold my dreams and make them reality. You have made me who I am, and I know what I will be. Yes, I can rejoice, for You hold my future and You know my destiny, Lord. You are the answer and hold all the answers to why. No, it's never too late; for You are my reality, my hope, and all the answers to all I need to know—and all I need to know is because of You. It's never too late.

DEPRESSION

You hold my heart captive; I can't seem to release your hold. You invade my thoughts and paralyze my will. Even when I don't think about you, you are a force that is always present. You have caused me to lose sight of my destiny and have been a killer of my dreams. Yes, I hate you, but I can't let you go. Will I ever be free? Can I let go? Will I ever be the person I was meant to be?

When my will becomes the will of God, my heart will be free, and no longer will your presence be a haunting force in my life. I can now see my destiny and my dreams are now a reality. Yes, now I can let go and let God. I am free, and I am becoming the woman God wants me to be.

PUSH

Rising from a pit, a place where the darkness always hovers over me, where my existence to be or not to be is the question. My survival has been diminished, for I feel like the prey that has been caught in a trap that won't be released. I see no light at the end of the tunnel, for I can't find the start of it. Pills, thrills, doctors—what does it all mean? After all this, I realize I must do this:

> **P - Pray**
> **U - Until**
> **S - Something**
> **H - Happens**

WORDS TO DESCRIBE MOM

My daughter wrote me this awesome poem on my fifty-eighth birthday. I would like to share it with you because as I am reading it now, I remember how I felt when she gave it to me. It was such a beautiful present.

Mom You Are:

Amazing – is how you raised me and my sister alone.

STRONG – with God on your side you did it all on your own

BEAUTIFUL – is for the peace you installed in us.

COURAGE AND PERSEVERANCE – is what you displayed hope is what you gave, we learn from you never to give up you told us it's OK to fall just get back up.

TOUGH AND GANSTA – is what you became when my behavior got rough, and you had to put your foot in my butt I think you now because I needed it so much. Because of the **WONDERFUL WOMAN** you are we are **WOMEN** of standards. There is not one word to describe you, you are an **AWESOME MOM THROUGH AND THROUGH.**

WHAT I KNOW ABOUT THIS MAN CALLED MY DAD

Growing up, I never knew my dad. I didn't know what he looked like or what he sounded like. I knew nothing about this man that was my dad. My mother told me what his name was—this was all I knew about him. One day, my mother called and told me that he had passed and where the funeral would be. I was curious, so I went to the funeral and heard all the wonderful things that people had said about him. I began to think about just what I knew about him, so this is where this poem came from.

> I didn't know about his warm touch or even if he
> loved me a little or very much. I didn't know if
> he was strict or even if he had firm ways. I didn't
> know of his comfort when I had bad days. I didn't
> know much of this man called my dad, but what
> I do know now is this man is dead.

TO MY DEAR FRIEND

You are a breath of fresh air in a time when things have become cloudy and dreary. I'm not sure what tomorrow holds, but knowing you makes right now okay. My heart seeks relief from the pain it feels, from the confusion it's facing; and hearing your voice helps me start on the path I need for recovery. I'm glad you are a part of my life, even if it may be temporary. Thank you for being a listening ear and a calming voice in a time when I needed both. Thank you, my dear friend.

TWO SOULS

I wrote this poem for a married couple that were dear friends of mine that were having twins. It truly was inspired by the spirit of God.

Two souls waiting to be born, waiting to be loved
and cherished. Two souls waiting for two souls to
be chosen for them and to be given. And God, in
His infinite wisdom, searched the world through,
knowing that there wouldn't be two souls worthy
of such gifts other than you two souls.

I KNOW IT'S LOVE

Thoughts of you invade my mind, and I have feelings of security and peace. As I think of your touch, your caress, I long to have you holding me close in the strength of your arms. I hear your voice, whispering words of tenderness and words of kindness. I think, I feel, I hear,

I KNOW IT'S LOVE

I WILL GIVE YOU PRAISE

In the midst my greatest pain, I will give you praise. When my joy has turned into sorrow and my laughter has turned into tears, I will give you praise. When I feel lost and all alone, I will give you praise. Because when my praise is greater than my circumstances, I am healed, delivered, and made free, so in all that I do and all I may go through, **I WILL GIVE YOU PRAISE.**

MY HEART

My heart is a treasure, why would I give it to someone who wouldn't treasure it?

My heart is full of love, why would I give it to someone who wouldn't accept that love?

My heart has promise, why would I give it to someone who couldn't keep a promise?

My heart is full of light, why would I give it to someone who's in darkness?

My heart is full of warmth, why would I place my heart in cold hands?

SEE ME

When I speak, see me. See my passion; see not my body's imperfection. Is my worth measured by my outer appearance, or is the inner me, my heart, my soul that makes me whole? **SEE ME!!** See my strengths and my weaknesses, my passions and desires. See my hurts and pains, my victories and gains. See my heart. See my soul!

SEE ME

DADDY'S HERE

My child, when you're in despair and all around seemed sinking sand, don't cry. Dry your tears. Daddy's here, Daddy's here. I know you're tired of going through the blows life is dealing you, but if you can, remember that hope is not gone, and, my child, you're not alone because always, your **DADDY'S** here.

This next poem has to do with a broken heart—when you love some-
one and they leave with no explanation, only a question: **WHY?**

> Why do I **FEEL** the sting of **LONELINESS** in my
>   heart?
> Why do I **CRAVE** the warmth of your embrace?
> Why do I **HUNGER** for the kiss that only your lips
>   can satisfy?
> When you are a part of me, why do I feel lone-
>   liness?
> Why do I crave, long for, hunger for love?

WHY?

JUST IN TIME

In the valley of despair, feeling no one really cares and feeling life has been a place of loneliness and cold, bitter headaches. Not knowing what to do, is there a place of hope or peace in my life? Just as I began to give into these feelings of doom—just in time, thank God—He sent me you. Your smile brings warmth to my cold existence, and your voice brings about a feeling of peace in a heart that was full of confusion. Yes, my friend, my sky is once again blue. For just in time, God sent me you.

WHEN, WHERE, HOW

My world is like a whirlwind—out of control, forever giving, never seeming to stop. When will it cease? When can my soul find rest, be quiet, find some peace? Where can I find hope when all seems hopeless? Where can I cast my cares when it seems no one cares? Where, what, how, I don't know. As I search my heart, the answer lies in my savior—the only one who can set me free from all that surrounds me and all that is in me. Only my savior can, and only my savior will.

WHERE IS THE LOVE

Is there a love worth finding? In my search for the answer, the question remains: is there a love worth finding? I have looked here, and I have looked there, not finding love anywhere: at home, work, church, and even on the bus. What I have found wasn't love. It was only lust. As I was giving up on finding the answer to finding love, it was on my knees that love found me. Yes, God so loved me that He gave His all—to love and to hold, to love unconditionally, to never leave me alone. A love that will last throughout eternity. Yes, there is a love worth finding. It's the love that loves you first, for it is the love of God.

INSIDE OUT

Inside out, the real, not a fantasy, where I stand naked and not ashamed, just free to be me. Or will I play the puppet on a string, living the would have, could have, should have, or what the world says I should be? My Father said I was made in His image. Inside out He's turning me, so I can be just me.

FROM MY DAUGHTER

This is a letter written to me by my daughter. It was written on January 10, 1992, and today is January 25,2023. I thought I would put this letter in with my poems because the wording of it is so poetic.

Dear Phillis Birmingham, I am writing to tell you that I appreciate you taking care of me. I am thankful for you being there for me and understanding me when I didn't understand myself. I know sometimes mothers wonder if they have brought their children up in the right way. Well, you have. Keeping me in a Christian environment through the years have done a lot of good. Sometimes I had the choice to do wrong, but I did not because in the back of my mind I could hear your voice telling me to do what was right. Many of timcs my upbringing has strayed me from harm and bad choices. I know sometimes you wonder if I ever pay attention or listen to your advice, I do, I can prove that because I am here today. Everyone makes mistakes and I forgive you. (And that's even if you think you have made any.) You may get on my nerves, but I will always love you. Keep on keeping on. You are a COLOSSAL MOM and don't let anyone tell you anything different! *

A Quality Product Molded by a Great Manufacturer.

In the next half of this book, I will be sharing quotes that the Father, Son, and Holy Spirit placed in my heart and mind.

I hope that in reading these quotes, the voice of God will speak to your hearts and give you the peace you've been praying for and answer the questions that your mind has pondered.

When you're in between a rock and a hard place, go to the rock, Jesus, and get directions.

The only time your opinion matters is when it's asked for.

If you live in the past, you will never be in the present, and you will never see your future.

A life without Christ is a life without hope, and a life without hope is just merely existence.

Weeping may endure for a night, but joy comes in the morning. Someone needs to know I see the sun coming up on the horizon.

When your atmosphere is changed because of someone else's pres-
ence, they have your power. Take it back by forgiving them. Let go
and let God!

God hates sin, not people. For God so loved the world that while we were yet sinners, God gave His life.

This is the day God has made—rejoice! Another day to be healed, delivered, and restored, to be free another day just to give Him praise for being alive just one more day.

The world may be in a recession, but the people of God shouldn't believe this report. We serve the God of unlimited wealth and resources.

If you don't resolve your past, it will follow you into your future.

When your future seems unsure, seek the one who holds and knows your future:

JESUS

When your situation is too big to handle, give it to the one big enough to handle it:

God

Whenever you are looking down and all you see are your feet, look up! See what direction your feet are taking you.

If you are going to worry, don't pray. If you're going to pray, don't worry.

Your life is like a puzzle. Please! Don't try to put people in it that don't fit.

Tomorrow is not promised to any one of us. Plan for your future, but don't forget to stop and smell the flowers today.

What good is your light if it is hidden? Shine bright so that all may see the glory of God in your life.

SHINE!!!

You can't truly say no to sin until you say yes to the one who has the power to forgive your sins.

When you don't know, go to the one who is all-knowing.

Most people don't keep their New Year's resolutions because they don't trust or know the one who does the resolving.

You can give someone your forgiveness without giving them your heart—or an open door back into your life.

When life has become too hard to bear, remember: God bore all on a rugged cross just for you. Give your all to Him.

What you think about yourself is what others will think about you.

God is the beginning and the end, the Alpha and the Omega. So why sweat everything that's in between? Trust God!

In all our weaknesses, God is made strong. The joy of the Lord is our strength.

Always be a blessing as you are blessed.

A broken heart can be mended even though its purpose was never to be broken.

ABOUT THE AUTHOR

Phillis is a woman of God who loves to serve her community. Her love for people is shown through her giving of resources to the community. Her encouraging words of faith have touched the hearts of many. Phillis's true passion and love come from her love for her family. She has two beautiful daughters, four grandchildren, and a uniquely special great-granddaughter. Phillis has preached at revivals and has brought the good news at different churches in her local area. Phillis has also been a praise team leader in several churches for several years. She was a backup singer for a gospel group singing in many states, then she became a solo artist singing at funerals, weddings, and anniversary parties. Phillis never thought that she would write a book, much less become an author, and this proves all things are possible with God. He goes beyond what you could ever imagine (Ephesians 3:20–21).